23

Ann.

The Dancing Sailors

Ann Pilling

Ann Pilling

August
2014

Indigo Dreams Poetry

Indigo Dreams Publishing

First Edition: Ann Pilling
First published in Great Britain in 2011 by:
Indigo Dreams Publishing
132 Hinckley Road
Stoney Stanton
Leicestershire
LE9 4LN

www.indigodreams.co.uk

ISBN 978-1-907401-62-6

British Library Cataloguing in Publication Data. A CIP record for this book can be obtained from the British Library.

Designed and typeset in Palatino Linotype by Indigo Dreams.

Cover design by Ronnie Goodyer at Indigo Dreams from the painting 'Dancing Sailors' by Christopher Wood used with permission from Leicestershire Museums and Art Galleries.

Printed and bound in Great Britain by Imprint Academic, Exeter.

for my children
and for my children's children

Acknowledgements

I would like to thank the following people for their thoughts on some of the poems in this collection:

Moniza Alvi, Susan Bassnett, Dawn Bauling, Julia Copus, Ronnie Goodyer, Benjamin Pilling, Joe Pilling, Thomas Pilling, Margaret Speak and Tamar Yoseloff, the members of Poets Meeting, London and the Settle Poetry Group.

Patrick Coyle for his work on the cover.

Benedict Rubbra for permission to reproduce his painting 'Benjamin and Thomas Pilling' and Jacqueline Banerjee for her photograph of this painting.

Dawn Bauling and Ronnie Goodyer (again) for all their help and encouragement at Indigo Dreams.

Some of these poems have appeared in The North, 14, Smiths Knoll, Staple and Yorkshire Journal and have won prizes or commendations in The Poetry Business Pamphlet Competition (twice) and The Yorkshire Open Poetry Competition (twice).

I am grateful to Leicestershire Museums and Art Galleries for giving their permission to my publishers to reproduce 'Dancing Sailors'.

CONTENTS

The Dancing Sailors

What is precious is never to forget
The essential delight of the blood drawn from ageless springs
Never to allow gradually the traffic to smother
With noise and fog the flowering of the spirit

Stephen Spender

Life

I have narrowed it to a plain place
less talk, less folk.

Today I watched a man walk down a field
along a rope of wall, its stones
still hugged by melting snow that spread
fish spines on the emerging green.

I have learned about finches and moons,
walked only by stars, marvelling
how their still, cold light felt warm to me.

The frost opens old cuts but here
I have no past and the land
arched between that life and this
is generous, like the speckled breasts
of these spring-hungry thrushes.

Rain

This rain has swilled all colour out of field and sky
grey sheep, grey grass, a new spring spews
grey foam up through a crumbling hole, the views
from our window are dull etchings *en grisaille.*
The river sizzles black, the beck boils brown,
trees litter the banks , a wall
of water smashes a bridge downstream,
leats thin as hair carve lines in the cheek of the fell.
I lie awake loving this rain, the print
of its hands on belly and thigh, the supreme
wet of it, the insistent beat. I want
only rain to enter me now, no warmth
of sun or moon or snow cover bedding me down
only rain and the fall of the rain.

Death by Water

Let me die near water, by the sea or a big river,
or by this little river that shallows out below the house
making a bar of sand where people swim, and dogs.

It tried to kill me once,
pumped its black water through me,
but when I went down for the third time
I heard someone call my name and the river
cast me up on a tiny shore, warm waves
caressed my feet.

I have done with battles. Let me be here
where the only swordplay is the river's under monstrous rain,
the long drops stabbing when its waterfalls
boil ochre and its bedstones,
all holed like ancient teeth, go under.

To be water, to be tumbled over and over,
lose feet, hands, breasts, be smoothed
to a fish shape, be mouthless and finless,
till what was me dissolves and turns river
and I'm teased out by hot sunlight,
gather on the surface,
become air.

Graves Near Whitby

October 2000

'Margaret, wife of the above, lies here.'
The slab all patched with lichen sags like an old bed.
Her mate was Zephaniah, mariner,
he had three wives.
Hannah and Ruth died young,
the third was left to care for his five sons
the day he perished in some northern sea.

They have been pulling bodies from the Kursk
and there are lovers' notes and children's flowers
and there are grainy faces pocked with tears
that stare like death's heads from the morning news.

Margaret, wife of the above, lies here
where gulls flap screaming over bitten grass
and the dark waters heave like Behemoth.
Kneeling, I brush some water from the stone
and flatten turf, so that her name is known.

Gimmer Lamb

It lies by the side of the road where the hill flattens
and you see the spread of the land for the first time.
It looks like a cast-off shirt though that blodge of black
could be a face. It is so still, a single bird
tears at the silence.

These fields are narrow, their stone walls
slung over the fell like cable, sheep
pebble Calva where its summit tracks.
course down the honey slopes like cream.
Nobody's come for the lamb yet.

Can't someone edge it on to the grass?
If it's left, what worms and birds don't eat
will dry out, whiten
to linen on a bleaching green, a walker
may grind it under foot

and the flakes,
caught in a balloon of wind,
will be tossed about, end up perhaps at the waterfall
where a man from a far country stands scattering ashes
in a place somebody loved.

Frost on Calva

Today the land shrouds itself, mist
lies heavy like a dead hand and we crunch
through coral fields of heather. These furred grasses
remind me of those woolly wires my father used
to clean his pipe. I loved
the scrunch of his knife round the bowl, the precise
tap of ash into fireplace, the wire
pulled through entire.

Frost heavy as this kills smell,
my father puffing, threading the air with something sweet,
the fragrance of soot itself. I'd wait
for its soft fall into the hearth, how it gathered on the fireback,
chose its time before dropping
in silent fissures into the grate. This slutchy lane
hardened to mirrors of rheumy glass
makes our boots skid. I limp back
towards village chimneys that write smoke
on skies the colour of tin.

Here the rooks wait in frosted elms
facing one way. Why do they wait? Calva
is lost behind white theatre drapes, their view
mere inches. I can go
no further with memory today no more than the rooks
can leave their branches. I am thinking
if I understood rooks more, I might understand love.

Equestrian Notes

To warm the bit in winter you can use
a small, non- toxic heater filled with gel.
To discourage iceballs, hooves may be treated
with non-stick cooking spray while peanut oil
will moisten feet after a drying wind.

If I'd owned a horse, I could have warmed the bit
by tucking it down between my new breasts,
I'd have attacked ice
with that gadget used for removing stones
on a boy scout's knife.
But I was a town child,
riding only on Sundays, always frightened
of meeting the bus.

Those big creatures,
terrifying and marvellous, felt close to the gods
and I have a memory I sometimes replay, two shire horses
clattering massively towards me down a Cheshire field
where I stood by a gate with my father
one hand in his, the other held out with sugar.

Festival Gulls

Seagulls, inland, crowd this brown city
their mastheads finials of high Victorian houses, their beaches
brown squares of trodden grass. In Charlotte Gardens
two do a floorshow, one high stepping
parades a big crust the other,
brown-blodged and whimpering trails after.
At night they mob the roof opposite, rip dreams up
with their raw crying while foxes
rummage in bags heaped shiny on pavements
like the crot of some Fringe monster.

I lie awake thinking of quiet country
of gulls that follow the plough, of foxes
threading through hedges with mouthfuls of feathers,
of us playing out in safe fields.

In that film *The Go-Between* the boy
saw limbs thrashing in an old barn,
now he gets it on line. We tiddlers
spied through a crack once
on the pink legs of our sister at it with Mr Steele
then went back to our own stuff,
squirrelling the puzzle away
as now, for later pleasure,
eventual need.

Boy

(after a portrait of Valdemaro Cristiano by Justus Sustermans 1597-1681)

I'd planned to go fishing, bunk off with Ned
the kitchen boy, then she grabbed me. She said
Sustermans was waiting in the white
sollar, a high room with the steady light
a painter needs. They dressed me in this lot,
yards of blue silk, papa's dress armour, not
the proper stuff he wore to fight
but thin plate, gilding painted on, each night
I pray for his soul. She has forgotten him.
They had scarce done with funeral rites when
this poufter turned up, honey-sweet, she sits sewing
watching him paint, she blushes, all unknowing
it's me he lusts for. Look at my lips, my hair,
desire for me is painted everywhere.
He's bird-beaked, his humongous nose nearly
touches his chin, he feigns indifference but really
he's rampant to bed me, I can see his hand
shake when he touches me, asks me to stand
more to the left, the look in his eyes. My mother
yawns, checks her timepiece, folds her work, no other
male attends on us. When the tower clock
strikes noon they dismiss me. Where can I walk
and not hear their dalliance? I see her
run from him down the avenue of limes where
he, pursuing, titters like a wench. Good Lord,
let him not make me his pimp or his bawd,
deliver me from this, from her drooling
over so vile a creature, from his fooling
with me at night. Let him not spill me.
Otherwise, kill me.

Kirkennan Wood

The frosted lawn's a paleish bluey green
the trees by Arthur Rackham, near the path
aconites make a rug, their yellowness
speared dark by one rogue crocus. Suddenly
I'm plunged into the darkness of the wood
where all the children played, I see my breath,
I count my steps, and listen to my heart.

It's lonely now, the glory of this place
is like a song played out on empty air
when no-one listens, three of us are dead
while one lies helpless in a hospital
and cannot raise her face to this great oak
lifting beseeching hands to the great sky.

Easter Garden

An Easter garden made with little hands
has stones for rocks, grape hyacinths in egg cups
stand for exotic trees, a handkerchief
is the Lord's graveclothes in the empty tomb.
Intrigued by all that's small I hunker down,
I stick my finger in and it is wet,
the rain has dripped its message through the roof
that death is death and there is putrefaction.

Home from the darkened church to this dark house
I beat the floor and scream and hear your voice
all full of stones and spit, I see you crawl
crab-like and old across the floor to bed.
At dawn the sun burns red like weals on skin
and birds begin their heartless little songs.

Firelight

I lie in the dark watching the flames
and try to separate their mild puttering from the faint
clash of the beck as it romps through the valley flats
at our field's edge.

Twice was it, or only once, you lugged
coal four flights up to my attic room?
The lump in my groin was the size of a pullet's egg.
Dr Boyd lanced it and I got a fever.

You brought boiled lemon drink,
coolish after your long clamber
from the kitchen with the tumbler
on a wooden tray.

'Hot glass
must rest on wood' you said.
'It won't crack if you do that.'
This was one of the wisdoms you gave me.

I see your face in the firelight,
your brows perfectly hooped
over your brown eyes. I smell you.
When I was ill you covered my face with kisses.

This coal has forged a strong heat.
I cross the floor and prise
the lips of the window apart to make a slit.
Cold comes through like a blackened tongue.

The Dancing Sailors

I see you walking on the beach at Douarnenez
your slacks bulgy with pebbles, shells in your hand
under a fierce blue sky, the blue
of Van Gogh's final cornfield spattered with crows.

You have gone too near the heaving sea
and I call out, you cannot swim,
you never grew up, you were Peter Pan,
you ran too fast for us to sew your shadow on.

In a square, sailors are dancing, the houses
are paper pasted on, a crooked church
peers through a gap while a chalk-cheeked man
waves his hat to some women in a window.

Whom the gods love die young, Vincent, Virginia,
the man who painted this, you – intense, beautiful,
savouring the sacrament of this hour
as you dance with the sailors out of the frame.

New Wife

It was like Hamlet how
her funeral baked meats furnished forth
your marriage tables,
'So quick' my sister said.

In the night our mother would always be there
knocking at the window like Cathy Earnshaw
crying to be let in and I'd say
'Go away, you can't come in,
you're dead. He's married Helena.'

And she'd trail off then with her little crumpled face
and we'd go on eating this perfect meal
at this perfectly round drum table
with these perfectly porcelain plates
and you'd say
'Oh children, be happy for my sake'
with your twisted smile.

That's why I never wrote and never phoned. That's why
when you rang me I learned to perfect the trick
of blotting your voice out by pressuring both my ears
to produce a funny screaming, high and shrill,
like the cry of something wounded on a road
that flaps back to life for a minute, then lies still.

Mary

When you were dead they stuffed you with spices
sweetened you up for the long lie
in the Abbey while folk traipsed by.

Were the embalmers gentle or did they
ram you like priming a cannon,
one last fuck from Philip who stayed away
as you lay dying?

I loathed your cruelties, that boy child
born while his mother fried at the stake
then chucked back to die, that fat
dripping from Cranmer's fingers to feed his own flames.

But you were passionate. It wasn't the knife
cutting your royal arms from your royal clothes
which did for you, it was the new wife

your mother's poisoner, your father's whore. She swore
she'd finish you too 'Were I to die for it' she said.
Did you clap when they chopped off that sleek Boleyn head?

When your womb swelled with wind you called it a child
church bells rang out, the waiting cradle
was hung with cloth of gold

till like a ripped bladder, you went flat again, wept
for your phantom infant, while behind their kerchiefs
your gentlewomen laughed.

Labour Day

for Katy

A fist smashed my door, slivering sleep, and I saw
my clothes in a glob on the floor
where I'd stepped out of them the night before.
Someone called for a cab through the street door
and they'd gone. I crawled
crabwise along the red strip to their room
and curled into the shell left by my son.

Katy came early, picking me over like a scrap heap, fingering
my grannyness, hair, nightie, the pearls
still in my ears and dived over, to find
a flatness where nobody was. Tears then, spouted cup
hurled across the room and her voice a deep soughing
Mummy.
The bed turned into a sea
where the waves of sorrow came big
rocking her little boat.

By cornflakes time we're talking balloons
blue for a boy, she's happy now, fighting George.
Grandpa's foursquare at the sink and I'm under the table
picking bits off the floor, of the earth earthy,
hearing the Underground trains, waiting for Mummy.

Green Woodpecker

Through our long window yesterday I saw this bird
big as a pigeon but narrower and green, two greens,
the belly a pale lime wash, the wings darker
and a jester's cap of a head splashed black and red.

It jagged the lawn with its dagger beak its feet
not moving, as if tethered to the spongy grass,
and its brilliance
lit the muck of November like a lamp.

We wanted it to come back, we watched for it
from our sealed house, holding our book of facts.
It is not seen in Ireland and its eggs are white, its young
are born helpless, and naked.

Last Train

This thick white light
shows up tomorrow's bristles on your chin,
I call it Rochdale light. When you first took me home
we sat in the same pitiless glare, there was a tin
with gold swirls on containing buns, your mother
stood rigid. I sat with my back against a wall.

I find a purple seat in the First Class,
nobody checks on this train, you stay
on the legal side of the glass, your mouth
ever so slightly pursed.

Your father wore a dressing gown because he had been ill
sucked on his fag and talked about Coloureds.
Your mother was small,
her voice loud, the clash
of the mill made the girls shout.

I want
no noise on this train and that soft
darkness we hunger for, very late at night.

Were you ever a child in that house?
Did they play with you ever? I pictured you
behind the door, waiting to grow up, counting
the years left to go before you could walk
down your grim, respectable street for the last time.

You wrote every week, tucked envelopes in
between your shirts and pants, orderly facts,
food in your hall of residence, your results,
stories of other blokes around the place.

But you never, I think, wrote jokes, or addressed
those letters in your wild and clownish hand
'The Cleghorns, Emma Street, Rochdale,
England,
The Universe, Space.'

Nature Study

He wasn't a man who thought about stars much
or enjoyed trees. To him
a walk was about keeping the map dry
and making good time. He was irritated
when I stopped to look at things, with him
it was all about covering the miles.

Ploddingly, every night, he lined up his small change
in neat columns on the bedside table
as his father had done before him, to stop
the pockets of his work suit bagging out.

But when his mother died
and I said in the night 'Where is she?'
he felt round for me in the dark and replied evenly
'I don't know, but wherever she is
I hope she's holding my father's hand.'

Birth Day

Time of gooseberries and cricket,
of Fylde potatoes and your father
telling the band to stop playing,
buying straw to spread under the window
where you lay sleeping,
that small, fastidious man who understood
only fragrant sheets and Nurse Aspinall's,
nothing of the shit and blood
through which you swam to be born.

And your mother, meticulous always,
you and your brother
at the start of any day spruced up and shiny
as if birthed by a carwash.

You were born on this day. I wake first,
see your pills counted out in neat rows,
your comb and toothbrush , your right hand
clutching the upper sheet in case someone takes it away.
Through all our years you have done this.
I leave you sleeping.

Dapper

On Sunday nights he shines his shoes.
A box in the wardrobe holds brushes and rags,
the sweet smell of the polish is like fruit.

Brogues, Oxfords and the lesser shoes
form a neat line by Mam's old rocker where he always sits,
today in a square of winter sun.

The humble tools of his trade are arranged
in a curve, with a surgeon's precision.
In his small hands the worn street pounders

are transfigured, his rubbing makes a gloss
you can see your face in, twigs through the window
swim up and pattern the jet-black boss of an office shoe.

Conker-brown lace-ups take him back
to the satchel they bought him that year
for the Grammar School, pencil and dinner smells

scythe away fifty summers. He can hear
Walter, who flapped into lessons in broken shoes
their soles patched up with leather scraps, see tears

on his goblin face. He shuts the box,
arranges coins and clothes for the morning,
goes downstairs.

The Laughter

One of us said something and you misheard
and through your back, washing up at the sink,
came slow, deliberate words about 'arrangements'
and we started to laugh, my friend and I, our cheeks
smoothed flat by silent mirth which took us,
blew us up and split our faces and set us rocking,
and if we swapped eyes we only laughed more.
It was awful because you, oblivious,
were still banging on at the sink.

My friend with her red hair looked beautiful her teeth
all white in her brown face, her eyes
all crinkled, she was crying with the laughter.
I was happy then, I was back
to the child I'd forgotten in a Lancashire classroom, sniggering
with Joyce on the back row, with nothing to go home to
but my mam and my tea and my homework and my ordered room,
no-one was dead and no-one was being buried.

When you came through from the sink we were still laughing,
Liz wiped her eyes, you cuffed me
with your neatly folded cloth and I started again and the laughter
floated off down the glorious valley
and settled, becoming light.

The Life of Objects

This carpet is determined to get into the next room.
We straighten it most weeks in line with the fireplace,
taking one corner each, like making a bed.

It's happy for about a day then it starts creeping
towards the bookcase in rich waves,
ink blue, the red of ox blood specked with white

where weavers cut their threads. It must know
that freedom's on the other side of the wall
and sunshine.

It was made
in a hot room overlooking a baked street
heavy with spice smells.

Abroad

Split off by sea, however warm
the folk, the sun,
eventual cold sets in

and a feather-thin blade
slits vertical down
till like cut fruit I fall apart

and the stain at the core
grows big, thoughts thicken
turn black

and my childhood terror comes back.
What if there was nothing
and always had been nothing?

Torn from the tree, I see me
bobbing about the universe. Is there
a ceiling, is there a floor?

Need I go back at all? I could be
that girl who went missing, the one
who tried swimming the Channel alone
and never came home.

from *The Tree of Man*

i Old Man Dying

Stan Parker dying saw a gob of spit
and said to the visiting preacher 'This is God,
this leaf also is God and these cracks in the path
they are God too,' and he died before the man
whose hair went up in even waves had reached
the end of the track.
                                        These kauris stand
four square in shallowed light their trunks
obligingly smooth for the loggers till they frill out
and shake their hair at the sun. He might have said
'This tree is God'. Certainly we trippers
sit long and quiet on the bench provided
in the presence of Tane Mahuta.

ii *Not Ray*

He's not Ray, he'd never kill puppies
or rob an old woman, he's pure gold.
He was like a little tree once, twin trunks
doggedly planted in rich soil, now I watch him
loving his own kid, eating him almost,
I who have kissed him with the kisses of my mouth.

He's on the same slide as me, soon he'll hear that boy
creeping along the parapet to meet his girl,
find the door shut.

The Grapes of Wrath

This book has been my friend. It has shielded me
from the man who sneered
from the girl who looked cruelly; in the peculiar
solitude of flight our beaked plane
parts clouds that fall away like new-washed hair
with the dustbowl seven miles down over whose red
they travelled, stuffed in their sagging truck, the mattresses
slung on top, the dogs and the buckets,
spyholes for the barrel of a gun and Granny's corpse
that they couldn't afford to bury.

Home in this little land
my brain is big with them still and I see again
their humble acts of intense love and how their maker
reached down through thirty thousand feet
to cradle them in his hands.

Against Gorse

It gashes the mild backcloth of sky and loch
with its brash gold, smears dim backroads
with gouts of yellow oil, the smell
is pear drops and a hint of human seed.

On Assynt it builds tremendous towers
the flowerheads shapeless, like smearings off fingers.
Lichening bony slopes it clambers skyward,
turns mountain.

And at sundrop when the land turns red
its burning bushes flame,
muster their thorns for clearances. Then
soldiers and angels square up with flaming swords
barring the way to Paradise.

Leeks

Before coming away I planted leeks,
sank two inch wells in good earth, Father's dibber
warm and familiar in my hand.

The soft walls crumbled in like mustard seed
so I dibbed again, firming them round,
then dropped the two-pronged seedlings fine as hair,
in the soft ground

and filled my holes with water from a copper can
and left them there, twelve snibs of green
flopped back on the dark soil, like things beheaded.

Here baked sand sears my feet, rocks dazzle;
walking on the tremendous cliffs near Ballintoy
I compose a card to my neighbour at home:

If the cats vanish and the leeks die
it's not your fault, no matter
in the great scheme of things.

But on the boat I picture them
erect and stubborn against the Dales' wind, feel them
plump up against our back wall
see my leeks grow fat.

Cherry Trees

Christine's path is covered with pink snow;
winds off Wetherfell have blown the petals slant
and thickened drifts already the colour of old roses.

The trees are like dancers,
the dolmen of the spine, the steel hold, the arms
that spring back into place when the music slows,

or monks in caves,
on upright watch when lightening rips earth from sky
or rocks, steady against big seas,

or a waterfall where one straight drop
shatters the pool below into bright petals
pearl, violet, indigo.

We could write our lives in flowers,
the daisied christening gowns,
the poppied pinafores our mothers wore,
the rose-sprigged wraps when they lay dying.

The Leylandii Hedge

How to describe its thisness
the pitch-green thickness of it, its absolute resistance
to any breaking of light. Hedges like these
make enemies, start wars, but it's only a question
of where the trees are planted.

In their right landscape
they could grow sheer and marvellous,
have the grave inevitability
of rocks, that rise up suddenly
out of a barren land,
giving the lost certainty,
shade to those who faint.

The Bay Tree

Winter did for it, the big snows;
it stiffened, turned its toes up, now
its brown leaves rattle like birdscarers, clatter
when I push past to the shed.

I could cut it down or smother it with roses
Rambling Rector, Paul's Musk, Albertine,
pretend it's a sculpture in copper
or let it sit there, being dead,

another reminder
of the way lust shrivels, friendship falls off,
that second when
a big love suddenly snaps, like bone.

Christening

Soro, Denmark

Today I think only of leaves,
burnt orange, black. The roofs
and timbers of this fairy town
are leaves – ox-blood, sienna.

Leaves slap my skin
like wet flags and I hurry in.
The frill of the priest is goffered
into small white leaves, he pours
her naming water from a shell.

She sleeps now
in the warm horseshoe of my arm
where once you put your head and wet
my sleeve. The leaves rain thick
on field and lake.

Twenty one years
of leaves cover the place
where your ashes lie. She has your face.
Today I think only of leaves.

Yorkshire Water

Did the grass scream when that red digger
first sank its jaws in
taking a big bite?

Did the perched pheasants
metallic bright against the fell perceive
those instant molehills as their right?

The land will heal but not one blade
will ever be the same or blow again
in the same place. At night

dark folds its wounds away, by day
they fester. I thrust
my seamed palms out of sight

thinking of old cuts and of how
nothing will quite obliterate
one deep, particular white line, try as it might.

Summer

Pulling weeds out after rain is lovely, the earth
opens like lips receiving a kiss and the stalks
yield easily as I take them from the ground. This grave summer
was full of rain.

Now swallows notch the wires like paper bows.
I must remember
that one great sunset, its red drops
heavy as mercury draining down the sky, its imprint
intense as perfume on a cotton square.

I must breathe deep and pocket it for winter, stuff
my hamster pouches full of summer
and the smell of grass.

This Field

I like this field, the way wind
fingers each blade
then ripples them up to the skyline in a single square.

I like the way
the lambs sit on their mothers' heads
and mob John when he turns up with their feed.

I like his even-handedness, tip sack, spread pellets.
From where I sit he's in a sea
foamed up by winds from Wetherfell.

I like it when Kath says
the trees are budding up, shows me
green pinpricks on a twig, with May half gone.

Here becks blether,
ewes get tupped: bap, sup, clowt, nowt,
words solid as Whernside.

When cold bites it's backendish and this field
will curl at the edges, fold in on itself,
wombing me in for the long sleep.

Haytiming

Through closed car windows all the way home
I smelt hay, its thin, sweet fragrance.
They worked all yesterday

and some already lies in long green bricks
on bristly fields, the rest like swathes of hair
still waits for the machine.

I step across our threshold
Virtute non Verbis spelt in tiles
and think of old Julys

of men who walked out of this house
to the Somme, to Caen;
up this lane a boy brought telegrams.

I climb steadily, going west,
to a shaved meadow where the dog
careers about, tossing the loose hay.

Below, the quilted land thrums with mowing,
while a horse big enough to pull gun carriages
sleeps in the shade.

Dales Fireworks

The vicar lights a touch paper and hurries clear.
A pause, as if the curtain's rising on a play,
then jetted from the flames bright rods striate
the plum bloom of the sky, harsh blues and reds
and showers of manic stars, the watching crowds
raise shiny little heads in serried ranks-
ball bearings from a childhood bagatelle-
and rapture breathes itself across the dark.

Old woman moon has seen it all before
and turns her face away, her head scarfed up,
stained grey on darker grey and sideways on,
seeing the show but hoping for the end.
She has learned patience though, she can wait till morning
for the trees again, and the barns, and the fell's mild clothing.

Cat

He lies under the snow
his grave cross-hatched with boughs
of ash chopped small, foxes go
across this land, one ear,
veined like a rose, folded
under my clod of earth.
A man died too, they shouldered
him cradled in wicker. Both
sleep sound in a white bed
heaped high by wind and now
flakes fall again, the hard
edges of grief softened by snow.

Soap Opera

You know they're acting, you can sometimes hear
scripts rustle or somebody stopping a sneeze,
but last night it was real, Rory
crying into the dark for his mother, daft
lies about heaven, Jennifer being brave.

Sleepless I've hit the garden at first light, my hands
full of deadheads. In the sycamore
a bird tunes up, its song
sweet as the morning, strong as grief.

On Waking

This newly minted hour, untouched by children
mouse-scrabbling at the door, carrying toys in,
waits for its imprint. I descend the stair
to breakfast in my burnished kitchen where
last night I knelt in Lego grit for stray
cornflakes and soldiers as they drove away.
Only for minutes does this pristine quiet
console. I thought I had done with riot
of guns and bathtime, I long for the sweet
tug of hands at my skirt, I am incomplete.

Painting Children

As arrows are in the hand of a mighty man; so are the children of the youth. Happy is the man that hath his quiver full of them. **Psalm 127**

When they were little Ben chose chequers, Tom
a soft red, they talked
with the artist about their clothes, they made
firm choices. Now
two men look out of the frame.

Ben's patched again with stripes and squares, Tom's
sleeveless, many-coloured coat glows quietly.
Ben's hands lie four-square on splayed knees, Tom's fingers
feel down like delicate roots.

He stares at something not in the room while his brother
looks as if there's a time limit; any minute
he might take off.

I want to unlock this picture, find a road
that takes me to what they were then,
what they are now.

Tom's hands make music, Ben,
so often sparring for a legal fist-fight, melts
into daftness when his kids roll into the room,

Blessed am I.
Blessed the man who has children.
Blessed is he whose quiver is full of them.

'BENJAMIN AND THOMAS PILLING' by BENEDICT RUBBRA

Stars

I meant to write about the apple tree
pricked out in little stars, about the day
you gave the lawn its first cut, how you said
it was all perfect, the grass
not dry not wet, answering your new blade
sweetly, like a bow across strings, the air
a-shimmer with spring and on your mown,
green double moons of turf
not one white petal.

Then, over coffee cups, Tom opened a paper
and read me the obituary of Irena Sendler
how she saved twenty five hundred Jews from the camps
all children, sedating them and packing them in boxes and sacks
sometimes in coffins, one in a toolbox,
getting the bigger ones out through the sewers under Warsaw.

She stared at me from The Times
apple-cheeked, anyone's Gran. Each side
of her head had a dint in, where they clubbed her. She saw
officers using skulls for target practice and
'a million other things that human eyes
should never have to see.'
As he folded the paper, a tear
squeezed out of his eye, shiny in the kitchen light, and rolled
quite slowly down one cheek.

It is cold this morning and there is
some yellow where you mowed. The apple tree
has shed its first white stars, they lie
like tears over the grass.

The Tinnygongle Stores

Along a sandy lane, by some old pumps,
we met it, spilled across the sketchy grass
like someone in an accident, with clumps
of mopheads, bowls and buckets, squares of glass
heaped up outside, the doors festooned with fixtures
for bathroom shelves on strings while buckets clinked
in the Welsh wind , Pears Soap and dolly mixtures
fuse wire and hen wire subtly interlinked.

Oh, butter off a slab, sugar in dark
blue bags, oh seaside pail with pirates on,
I shut my eyes and paint my past, lawnmowers,
hair pins and glue in little beads, that stark
woman with scraped-back hair shaking the tin,
my childhood done in Reeves's watercolours.

Basilica

Naxos, September 2010

Stubby, brown as the brown grass,
it sits in the olive grove like a grandmother
spread round with bags and children.

Lizards guard it, sunning their candy stripes
in the downstroke of A for Apollos,
in a fragment of days before Christ,
a marble slab let into a wall.

The door is shut but I want to see more
than a smudge of angels through a slit,
to stand in its hunched interior, be washed with cool light.

This island has layers, the Cycladic idols
with their long faces, the invisible gods
of field and sky, Zeus and Persephone, Emmanuel.

The ghosts edge past me, leaving their goats and donkeys
under the trees, pass through the hooped doorway
with offerings of wine and olives and rough bread
to a place where prayer has been valid.

Gone

Now you have gone who can I thank
for today's river, tonight's stars?
I used to see your hand in everything
and when I couldn't sleep
I took that hand and held it against my face.

This day
feels like the first of spring, our collared doves
spread opal wings over the grass, the rookery
is blotched with birds, willows
show through a mist of green. Such days
are like a gift but how can I give back
now you have gone?

There has to be another way to look at spring. Winter
was hard and the churchyard's fat
with its new-mounded dead. Under a hedge
the claw-clutched corpses of small things lie
killed off by unusual cold. This return
of warmth to the land I could view as heartless now
heartless the song of chicks and the patter of mice
which in due time will curl like withered leaves.

But you were never heartless, a god
who gave no answer because he was the answer, a god
who wound up the world and left it to tick.

I miss you.

Watching for the Otter

One languid afternoon we watch for the otter, peering
into the greeny stream, eyes cocked
for whiskers to break the surface, the sleek of a head.
Otters are shy, I tell him.

In his book *lutra lutra*'s as stiff as a post
long belly whitewashed, big tail curled flat
as if steadying a rickety parasol.

His eyes slide down the page
to badger and wolverine. Back in the sandpit
I'm Saul, he's Goliath, a fox
comes into it somewhere.

While he sleeps I sit on by the thick water, wind
rattles the poplars, butterflies
have given our spent lavenders a second flush
of small white flowers

when something splits the skin of the stream, a bruise
slicks the water then
it's flat as lily plates again.

He is not here but he has been this way,
like something pushing through wet grass,
leaving a shiny path. At dusk,
and in the morning, I watch for the otter.

My First Owl

What is it about owls? Why is the memory
of my first owl etched with the same fierce acid as the day
they took away my mother?

We've got owls here, a family of them
squats in the Spanish chestnut. From the house
they look like binbags caught in its branches.

It's the owlness of owls, their bespectacled faces,
their bigness, the way, as dusk starts creeping
delicate as a cat, they glide silently to their watching places.

Let my last journey
be by owl, my face
snuggled into its feathers, my fear

stilled by its wingbeat. Then sleep,
that small, clean gap before eternity
opens like dawn, and we sink to rest.

Notes

The opening quotation from Stephen Spender comes from his poem 'I think continually of those who were truly great'.

Graves near Whitby – p14

Kursk, a Russian submarine, sank in the Bavents on 12th August 2000, with one hundred per cent loss of life. They started pulling out bodies in October the same year.

Boy – p19

See 'Prayer Before Birth' by Louis MacNeice.

Kirkennan Wood – p20

'Kirkennan' in Dumfries and Galloway, SE Scotland, has been a family holiday home for three generations.

The Dancing Sailors – p23

'Dancing Sailors' was painted by Christopher (Kit) Wood in 1930. Later that year he committed suicide, as had Vincent Van Gogh. Virginia Woolf and my mother were to follow.

Mary – p25

Mary Tudor, daughter of Henry VIII and Katherine of Aragon, and wife of Philip of Spain, called 'Bloody Mary' for the savage executions of protestants during her reign.

Abroad – p35

'Swim the Channel' was a four minute tragic-comic sketch by Victoria Wood in her series 'Victoria Wood as Seen on TV'.

from *The Tree of Man* – p36

a novel by the Australian Patrick White, 1955.

i Kauri are the oldest trees on earth and Tane Mahuta 'the god of the forest'.

ii Ray was the no-good son of Stan and Amy Parker.

Haytiming – p47

In Swaledale and Wensleydale, North Yorkshire, making hay is traditionally called 'haytiming'. My home in Wensleydale has the motto *Virtute non Verbis,* (by deeds not words) spelt in tiles across its threshold.

Painting Children - p52

Benedict Rubbra painted Benjamin and Thomas separately as young children, then together as young men. See 'Benedict Rubbra: Point of Balance' Jenny Pery, 2008.

Basilica – p56

'where prayer has been valid' - see 'Little Gidding' (Four Quartets) T S Eliot.

Watching for the Otter – p58

'He is not here but he has been this way' : a description of the mystery of the Holy Spirit, 'Prayer', Simon Tugwell.

DANCING SAILORS by CHRISTOPHER WOOD

Indigo Dreams Publishing
132, Hinckley Road
Stoney Stanton
Leicestershire
LE9 4LN
www.indigodreams.co.uk

Papers used by Indigo Dreams are recyclable products made from wood grown in sustainable forests following the guidance of the Forest Stewardship Council.